CONVERSATIONS *with* MARY

Also by Jamie K. Reaser

Coming Home:
Learning to Actively Love this World

Winter:
Reflections by Snowlight

Wild Life:
New and Selected Poems

Sacred Reciprocity:
Courting the Beloved in Everyday Life

Note to Self:
Poems for Changing the World
from the Inside Out

Huntley Meadows:
A Naturalist's Journal in Verse

Courting the Wild:
Love Affairs with Reptiles and Amphibians

with Susan Chernak McElroy
Courting the Wild:
Love Affairs with the Land

CONVERSATIONS
with MARY

WORDS OF ATTENTION AND DEVOTION

JAMIE K. REASER

TALKING WATERS PRESS · *Stanardsville, Virginia*

Cover and text design by Jason Kirkey
Cover art © Meredith McKnown Peyton/Peyton House Portraits

ISBN 978-0-9968519-1-6
First Edition 2019
Talking Waters Press
Stanardsville, Virginia

"I'm curious if you have a ritual or practice that you
use to prepare yourself to be mindful on your walks
and wanderings that appear so beautifully in your
poetry. How do you kindle the kind of gaze that is
able to take in all the things that you do?"

HER ANSWER
"No ritual, no preparation.
Just attention and devotion."

APPRENTICE

Poets apprentice to the very first word.
Mastery arrives at the end,
but it is never ours to keep.

Humility
Felicity

CONTENTS

THE BLUE RIDGE MOUNTAINS, VIRGINIA

We take walks in the driveway in the late afternoon,
the cats with their tails raised and paws touching the
clay ever so lightly. We stop at the crossroad of other
people's comings and goings with speed and
forgetfulness, and turn. We have butterflies at the
flowers to adore.

Cicadas and katydids, taking their turns, perform
from the same orchestral score—summer. The cats
don't seem to care much about that, but I do. And,
my watch confirms the waning of this kind of simple
thirty-minute joy. There are transitions, but nothing
pauses for us. Attentiveness is the only way to love.

Some of the birds see us and scold me for the company
I keep, but this is a ritual about more than they know.
How few of us ever get to walk beside a soul beckoned
into our company by devotion? These mountains,
blue in humid haze, know this of me. But, that's a secret
I am keeping.

We long for connection; solitude endures.
We make plans, but the world is too much for that.
There was a roll of thunder, but no lightning.
We walked back to the house.

Satisfied with briefly knowing the world,
the cats were back on the kitchen counter again,
wanting their dinner. My thoughts, already tightening
around the tasks ahead, opened the can. The sacred
resides in knowing that this isn't going to last
forever.

The River Styx, Ohio
The River Styx, Ohio, and Other Poems

WHAT WE WANT FROM A FLOWER

Tell me nothing,
and I won't believe
you. Within you
there is longing,
something

that you want from
a flower, maybe it
isn't a fancy thing,
but I'll bet it is
profound. Life

changing, maybe.
Have you thought
about this? I hadn't
until today. I'm

thinking about
it now, how I want,
no, expect, flowers
to make things
better. They do. Isn't

this interesting? I wonder
what a flower wants,
no, expects, from
me.

What We Want
Blue Horses: Poems

A MOOSE IN THE RAIN

She thinks *the face of a moose is as sad*
as the face of Jesus. But, Jesus didn't look
sad when we met. And, the moose, he
was, I'd say, fully accepting of his awkwardness.

All my life, I've been trying to be that moose,

though, until now, I wouldn't have said "moose,"
maybe "duckling," because that's the story I
remember being recited to me, repeatedly, during
an awkward childhood; they, perhaps, thinking it
a salve, but I've never looked and seen a swan
looking at me,

so when I saw him there, his fleshy proboscis
lipping shrubbery in the pouring rain of Denali,
his body his own and soaked in its true nature,
I thought:

"This is magnificent! I am a moose."

Some Questions You Might Ask
House of Light

THE TREES SPEAK

Those who can hear the trees speak have never
had a thought of loneliness. What they know
is joy, and something of grief.

Trees tell amazing stories. Stories told by
generations of trees. They pass them along.
Wherever it is you stand now, there is a tree
that knows the story of that place.

How do I know these things?

I'm crazy enough to ask. That's all that
this delightful world requires of us:

to be crazy enough.

Do the Trees Speak?
Felicity

THE ENCOUNTER

I heard it at the front door.

The front door!

This great scream.

It was, in fact, a scream,

And it begged me to
come running,

running on a large-shoed foot
of wonderment
and another of fear,
striding, one after the other.

What could it be? This thing that screams.

At my front door!

And there he was.
    I had asked for him only days before.

And there he was.

I grabbed my camera and headed after him.

Slowly, but fast too.

He looked back,
making sure I was there,
and sauntered.

He sauntered down the driveway away from the cabin.

No. He loped.

He loped down the driveway, picking up
his big (magnificent!) paws and letting me
count the pads below
and memorize their shape
and their position so that I'd know his signature
anywhere;

In mud maybe, or snow. By the creek. I'm sure.

And there he was.
There we were.

And, then, he leapt to the right,
bounding into thick greenbrier and up the mountain
slope he was gone.

He didn't ask permission to leave.
Or, even gesture a "Goodbye."

He was informal. The wild isn't polite.
No one has ever told it to be, and it wouldn't be anyway.

But, there he had been.
And, there we had been. Together. Long enough
to know of the existence of the other.
Long enough to be able to say we had
an encounter.

How would he describe it?

Long enough for me to feel blessed
and him to feel whatever he felt.

I could claim that my prayer was answered.

I certainly can't deny it.

I had so wanted to see a bobcat.

THE LATE SUMMER DAY

I had many things planned for this precious life,
but I've since learned that planning is a binding,
a tether, a grip that, when taken up in earnest,
keeps us from freely roaming all of the grand
possibilities. Like old mountains, and cricketed
fields, and long, edgy shorelines.

Now, not knowing is my practice. It works okay.
On most days, and some nights. The dark-skied ones.

I think that mystery is the only medicine for the
wild soul that nags at the feet restlessly;
predictability and sameness pain its true nature.

This I understand.

Summer is going somewhere, but not in any way
that we can imagine. I could tell you things:

A battered white moth will lose itself to
the chill surrounding a porch light.

The sunflowers will hang their heavy
finch-beaded heads until their bodies snap
and they lie there, welcoming the molds.

The bird voice that was your awakening for
four straight months is gone, but you will be
confounded as to why you overslept.

And the bear, the bear cares about nothing
more than its belly. You'll come around a
sharp curve in the trail and, startled by

form and scent, you'll halt. The bear's head is in
thick duff and acorns. You don't matter.

Keep walking.

But that won't be it. It will be something else
entirely; more bold and more subtle.

Yes.

I want the next day to be that for me.

THE BLACK SNAKE

When the black snake arrived,
with her innate knowing,
in the bed of straw in the barn,
the farm dogs said, "No! No! No!"
and were ready to pounce,

But I said, "Yes!" and "Leave it!"
which they understood, turning
their wide black heads and brown
eyes to me, perplexed: "What?"

I had heard death ask for permission.
There were wood rats in the rafters
under rough sawn lumber and dust.
Death was the snake. Up the barn wall
she went, two dogs watching. Me too.

I love the woodrats. I love the snake.
I love the dogs. I'm learning to love
the gut-wrenching vulnerability that
is death fully agreed to, fully witnessed,
fully occupied. Isn't it the terrible,
but necessary love?

There are destinies that need us
to actively partake in them. I think we
are all living them. I think these times
are living them too. How hard it is to say
goodbye, to yell out: "Yes!" and "Leave
it!" What else are we being asked to
let go on its destructive way?

Ask a snake with a thick mid-section
to tell you the story of her good fortune.
How happily she will tell it. Can you
accept her joy?

Can you find your own?

The Old Poets of China
Why I Wake Early: New Poems

THE PALE MISTS

We must have been two of those old poets of China. I remember being in good company, sitting on a rough-cut bench, smoking long pipes through streaming grey beards, high in the cloud-cloaked mountains. They say that masters come in many forms. For us, I think that it was the pale mists. How they taught us to see what we couldn't see. How they taught us to write about unspeakable things.

The Old Poets of China
Why I Wake Early: New Poems

THE RIGHT PLACE

Some know what they want. Yes, maybe it is to be among the trees.
Or, to be in a garden in some place where a garden is an act of
defiance of something.

You advise: *Try to find the right place for yourself.*

But I don't think that's it. I think we want to be found. I think we
need to be found. That's harder than finding, don't you agree? To be
found, you have to be still. You have to be vulnerable to something
that wants you. It could be dangerous. You're lucky if it is.

People are not alone, but they are lonely. The body has forgotten
what it is made of. So has the spirit. I watched a meteor shower last
night. I'm not going to go into the details, but that's some of the stuff.

Here is a good place to be, especially when I take notice of the fact
that I'm breathing and muster the gratitude for it. When was the
last time you heard your breath? We were given ways of knowing
that we are alive and well.

When I talk to the gods, they don't say much. Why utter lies? I think
they are well aware that we are not yet ready for the truth. It's an
interesting thought, that.

The experts say that when you are lost, you should just stay put.
Sit. Wait. I haven't been particularly good at waiting. Maybe that's
because, up until now, I hadn't really realized what I was waiting for.

Leaves and Blossoms Along the Way
Felicity

ANSWERS FOR MARY

Yes!
I saw it, its bill like the compass needle
which is wholly committed to truth.
I knew of its pertinence the very moment
my heart took flight.
You see, beauty isn't for figuring.
Beauty exists only for the embodiment of beauty
        a holy union of form and essence
to be lived into the world like
the sacred contract between mated swans.
And oh yes,
with this,
I've changed my life.

Swan
Swan: Poems and Prose Poems

CARRYING THE TURTLE ACROSS THE ROAD

In the road
was the most determined
turtle I have ever seen.
Rushing, in its turtle way,
to get to the other side,
nails raking the asphalt,
dome shell rising
like a home built
to carry endless time and
possibility and
impossibility too.
My brakes screeched,
my eyes darted,
my heart prayed,
my body flung itself
out the door,
my right hand grabbed,
my mouth apologized,
my foot hit the accelerator.
What are our lives worth
if not for the keeping of
other lives?
In the morning light of
a Sunday, I parked
at the edge and carried
her unceremoniously across
the road, sending her on her
same way with blessings. Was
this too much? Was it
not enough? She didn't
look back. I thought maybe
she didn't understand that
I had disrupted her

certain death. I thought,
for a moment, about how
much thanklessness drives
this world.

But, then, I kept going with
my thankfulness for life.

CHOICES

There are choices that long to be made.
Like, being who you are born to be,
Or, living something resembling a life, all the way through.

You have a soul, don't you?
You have a limited number of days in this body, don't you?

What good is it to inhabit this place if you don't
inhabit your life? I'm asking you to save the world.

Moments
Felicity

HIDING EASTER EGGS

She was terrible at it.
We'd find the pastel-colored, plastic
eggs filled with stale candy months,
maybe a year or more, later.

Behind the curtains.
Under the sofa cushions.
Beneath the lamp shade.

Perhaps a family dog would eventually
alert us to them, or we'd get around
to cleaning, or be looking for something
necessary that we'd misplaced.

We'd say, "Count them first!"

We'd say, "Make a map!"

But, it never happened and we'd be
left to joke that we had a particularly
senile Easter Bunny.

We can lose things so easily.

🐦

"Be attentive," counsels Mary.

🐦

Tomorrow, we'll hide eggs for the kids.

Across the green lawn.
In the trees and shrubbery.
On the jungle gym.

When all is said and done,
the baskets filled and
the sugar coursing, we'll pretend
to have lost at least one.

We'll say, "That's in honor of
Grandma Billie." And, they'll
think us nuts.

It'll be our way of being attentive.

WHEN MEN SELL THEIR SOULS

"When men sell their souls,
where do the souls go?"

It's an important question,
if we want to get them back.

And, we should, you know.
There are good reasons to do it.

❧

I have a deep fondness for hollow
trees, they welcome so much to live
within them: a screech owl whom I
have known personally and, on my
farm, there is an old black locust filled
with thick honeycomb and sweet,
golden honey and so many bees that
the tree hums and vibrates under a
many-lined palm laid gently upon the
vertical running bark. We keep each
other secret.

But, hollow people, they don't let
the lovely things in.

❧

I find myself spending more and more
time with trees.

Sand Dabs, Four
Winter Hours

SUNFLOWERS

There are many kinds in my garden.
I grow them as teachers.

I love them; how they embody joy
in a way I find curious and, on days that
I won't tally,
elusive.

What is it like, I wonder, to be the thing
on which soft bumblebees alight (they are soft,
I have petted them) to collect their dusted gold,
or butterflies—the fritillaries, sachem skippers,
and monarchs—nectar their brave, dazzling lives,
or a differential grasshopper sits long enough to
complete his survey and report unto God
about the things going on down here?

If I chose not to plant them, it wouldn't be such
a happy garden, and this could be one of those
unlived lives that catch your eye at check out.

It's true.

I'll tell you that summer has gone and they—the
sunflowers—are now bent at the waist by
the weight of their heads, looking
like skinny monks at prayer seeking
emptiness
as fulfillment.

This is when I begin to listen most carefully to the soft
om resonating across the beds of straw at their feet.
Hear now, the wisdom gained from two months
of standing still,

and in the last breath of a well-seasoned death
that I record in my cells,

a vow of endless servitude:

"Now, I shall feed the birds."

The Sunflowers
Dream Work

THE COYOTE

We met in the light of sky and earth,
thick snow slowing time and making each
equally apparent to the other. My body
quivered as if finally found by the beloved
who could at once adore and devour me.
Suddenly, I was a maiden in the wilderness
taken by my animalness, caught in the
throws of an allurement from which
I did not want to run. But, he ran. He
lifted his magnificent body into the air
and leapt from my life, leaving me there
raw, with his ghost and my hand in his
tracks. I thought, now I understand,
now I know why Coyote is despised so.
We humans are the self-banished. The
long-time residents of the lonely place
of silenced voices. But, the call is there.
He is the terrible desire that we go
on killing.

Coyote in the Dark, Coyotes Remembered
The Truro Bear and Other Adventures

HOW MANY MORNINGS

How many mornings have I risen and forgotten that
rising is a gift? The sun streaming through my window,
or a grey horizon, or rain pelting the metal roof: gifts.
And, the bird song or just bird banter. The dogs begging
with their big brown eyes to be fed the same kibble
they were fed yesterday and all the days before. Gifts.
Mornings deserve tenderness, a caress of gratitude, a
little recognition that nothing is promised. I think that
we could learn to say, "Thank you!" to the sunrise
and keep the world alive.

How Many Days
Swan: Poems and Prose Poems

I BOW DOWN

I bow down.
I bow down to the sky that oversees
the liars and the truthsayers.
I bow down to the earth that conveys
the rich and the poor.
I bow down to the child that will lead
tomorrow and the child that leads
today and the child that must become
an angel because we won't follow
the children otherwise.

What I stand for is that which
I bow down to:

that which says we're not done
yet, there's a lot more to learn
to love.

Am I Not Among the Early Risers
West Wind

27

CRAZY PEOPLE

I can feel a poem's sting and sometimes its hope.
And, frequently, its surprise when it arrives like
all truths do, from someplace other than my
busy-bee of a head.

Some call on muses. I suppose that I've known a
few. Some are gentle, humble souls. Others brash
and quite self-important.

Generally, though, I just make a place for what is
already there, for what has been waiting for,
perhaps, a very long time for human attentiveness.

A moment of listening.
A moment of looking.
A moment of recognition,
and some degree of wonderment.

"Oh, my, isn't that....?!"

There are words lingering in the ethers, always.
Most of the ones I meet, tell stories. Usually,
my own. It can take a while to know them.

Please believe me:

It's okay to hear things and see things that
other people don't see and hear.

The world needs more crazy people.

It does!

Good Morning
Blue Horses: Poems

THE BLACK WALNUT TREES

When I arrived here things
were not as I had expected,
not at all, truth be told.
On my first night, I slept
out on the deck, under the
stars and the arm of a tree.
In the night, she came to me,
a bright shining she who
was the tree and she said,
"I know why you are here. The
land called you here." With
that, she left, but I did not.
One day, a man came up the
drive in an old rust-bottomed
pick up. He thought me a fool.
"Ma'am, I see ya got these big
ol' trees, dangerous, gonna fall
on yur place. I'll cut 'em fer ya,
even carry 'em away, cheap."
I know a thing or two about
being swindled, and also how
to talk like I'm from a place.
"Sir, ain't nobody gonna touch
my black walnuts! Not today,
not ever. No, Sir, they ain't.
Now, git!" He understood me.
The truck bumped its way back
down the drive at, quite remarkably,
twice the speed it had arrived.
He hasn't called on me since.

So, the black walnut grove still
extends its arms, still embraces
my little cabin, still embraces me,
still knows secrets that
I haven't yet learned
of myself.

The Black Walnut Tree
Twelve Moons

STANDING THERE

I happened to be standing there.
Initially, it didn't seem like a particularly
special moment or a special place, although
there is something special about everything
and everyone, it's just that some people
keep what is most special secret. I know.
But, there I was, making one of those
silent prayers that you make in the woods
because it's your cathedral and there it came,
wide wings low across the trail and whoosh
to the toe of my boot, big, dark saucer-eyes
looking up, straight into mine, locked for an
eternity-second. There was blood on the
tip of its beak. Interesting, I thought. Without
words, it said, "I claim you." And, that was that.
Some prayer was answered. I'm not sure
which one. Maybe, it was all of them.

I Happened to Be Standing
A Thousand Mornings

THE CROWS

The sky was blue today, beautiful, and
there were crows in it. Black. Iridescent.
Raucous.

I know that you've seen crows
too, though you've said you didn't
and in not seeing them didn't see
the things that we might prefer birds
don't do—like putting their sharp beaks
into dead things and eating them
in a way that reminds us of our
sorrows.

Dark angels get little welcoming.
But, imagine! What great courage it
takes us to earn our wings.

Crows
The New Yorker

A SNAKE IN THE HAND

My parents decapitated every snake
they saw. I remember watching severed
heads and severed bodies writhing,

separately,

in the grass. The mouth would open and
close, open and close. It was pink inside.
Maybe, black.

When I was old enough to read field guides,
my parents got in trouble. Big trouble.
According to the books, there were no
venomous snakes where we lived. None.
Every single species was harmless. Actually,
they did good things.

I was not happy.

I laid down the law. "You aren't allowed to
kill any more snakes!" My declaration was
non-negotiable and backed by facts. Plenty.

That was the day that I learned to stop
trusting everything adults said and did.

The next snake that I encountered was
a garter snake—a large female. I reached
down and picked her up, gently placing the
fingers of my right hand behind her narrow
head and supporting her sleek body with
my left hand, just like the books said to do.

Then, I went to find my parents.

I was told that 'it' was not coming into the
house. Ever. But, I was given a playpen-sized
box that an appliance had arrived in earlier
that week.

The snake and I spent most of that day
on the back patio in that box with grass
that I pulled and worms that I caught.
She ate a big one. It was still wriggling
when it disappeared into the universe
inside her.

I learned a lot about snakes that day,
like how easy they are to love.

I let her go.

And, the next day, I went down to the
brook that ran patiently behind the house
– Harrison Brook –
where I knew northern watersnakes
lived in holes at the top of clay banks.

I waded in waist deep, causing water
to separate at my left hip and embrace
me before flowing onward, and waited for
them to swim by – going to or from their
streamside apartments. When they came
my way, swimming, I'd put my hands in the
water under their long undulating bellies
and gently lift them up. Then, I'd get
bitten. It never hurt much, but it did
draw blood. Sometimes.

I did this again and again, until they
trusted my particular touch. Then, I'd sit
with one or two on the sandy shoal at
the turn in the creek and just look at them
and talk to them. I think they said things
to me too, but I don't remember
what, exactly.

All demons can be befriended this way.

The snake in my hand, right now, is a lovely
ringneck, steel gray with a golden belly and
collar. She's silky smooth and elegant,
looped around my thumb and forefinger.

I relate to scales in much the same way that
religious people relate to beads. Holding her
is an act of prayer. But, what is the prayer?
This is my question. I think that it is a good one.

I think, perhaps, I'm still praying for those
decapitated snakes. Or, maybe, I'm praying
for people. Decades have passed. I'm still
clear about who is harmless. But, it seems,
much of the world is not.

Searching for Snakes
House of Light

THE BLUE IRIS

But, what if it is the blue iris?
What if that is all we need to speak
to God, or the gods, or some other
form of the sacred?

I try to pay attention. I piece words together.
This is prayer, yes. But, more so, it is ceremony.
I want to hear another voice. I want a reply.
I want to know that I'm not alone and that
all of this matters.

May I put it in a vase? May I decorate my home
with it? It is beautiful.

Could I be worthy of something
that I love?

Praying
Thirst

THE CAROLINA WREN

It is daybreak and the Carolina wren calls
out from the thick of old boxwoods that stood
around a log cabin and someone else's lives with
a loud, cheery greeting that has defied the
intricate telling of at least two poets.
They won't sing it either. But they know how to
pay attention, appreciate, and praise a thing. Anything.
And this is what he is doing too. This bright chortle
must be praise. Maybe it is for daybreak. Maybe
spring. Maybe simply the fact that he has a song
when so many have forgotten theirs. It could be
that it is about tasting a morning seed, or little
jumping spider, or simply that it is with song
that he tastes this life. Poets can do the same thing
with words. We won't starve. Praise satiates. I want to
believe that we all have some way of coming alive each morning
and care to do it, to taste this life, and have the courage to
say there is something holy inscribed in all of it. It's not
necessarily about bread or wine. It doesn't require formality.
You can be rascally about it, like the wren, like
some poets. Guess which ones.
There is a wren in the boxwoods next to me.
I have a cup of tea. And, I'm so grateful
that I couldn't contain myself.

The Wren from Carolina
Why I Wake Early: New Poems

THIS IS SOMETHING

This is something we didn't plan,
and couldn't have.
This in unimaginable.
This is what beauty strives to be when
it shows itself in the world.
This is the beginning of something
we had already begun.
That's the way it feels.
This is one night and one morning
and something you said about
something more.
This is absent the old rules that
have been keeping the world
too small.

What This Is Not
Felicity

ROBINS IN WINTER

Robins in Winter
They said to me: "Stay strong, the
cold days will pass. Someday
soon, you can come with us to
forage for worms. There will be
no more need for this difficult
search for the very last of the
dried berries."

I had never before longed for
worms. But, suddenly, there I
stood, realizing that all I
wanted in the world was the
soft company of a worm. And,
my hand, was empty.

Starlings in Winter
Owls and Other Fantasies

THE SECOND SNOW

It wasn't the first snow of
the season, the second, but
it called for at least as much
reverence, for all attention
one could give to it.
It started in the night,
greeted the morning, and wanted
the day as its own, and took
it in silence and prettiness. The dark
tree skeletons held it up, turning
themselves into many-winged
angels, revealing their true nature
to those who can utter something
more whimsical and deeply honest
than, "It is snowing!"
On days like this, I want to find my
way back to all the snows I've seen,
and all the people who were there
too. There are conversations that
never happened under that thick
white blanket, but there was
laughter too, and that unique familiarity
that snow brings, much the way that the
moon brings familiarity, and the darkness,
and the sun and stars, though somehow we humans
still remain lonely. Often. I want to gift questions
about loneliness into the world; how we came
to abandon the good company of magic and
retreated into the world of rationalized noise. But,
not now. Now, I want to let myself be claimed
by the beauty of the snow – the second snow – because
I've already found the answer.

First Snow
New and Selected Poems [Volume 1]

THE SOFT ANIMAL

The soft animal of my body loves the deep
cup of the nest, but also the edge of the nest,
and the nothingness that is everything on the
other side. I am not built to love one thing or
one way, or limit myself to loving one world.
What is too small must be broken through or
left behind. At times, I've needed to do both.
Right now, right now, I just want to sit with
the last moment, the one, the last one, before
I completely let go.

Wild Geese
Wild Geese: Selected Poems

IN THE WOODS

I take long walks in the woods, usually up and down mountain slopes. Usually alone. Alone in that I'm not in the company of another human. I'm never alone, really. I've known this since I was a little girl in braids. The forest is such good company. It can hold you in ways that people can't, even those who would want to. You can be invisible there, yes, but you can also be seen. I think this is important, this being witnessed. I think we have forgotten about it, witnessing. It is a testament and a salve. It used to be initiation. All the while the birds are singing, we miss it. On the branches of the trees:

"I see you. See me."

Instruction.

How I Go Into the Woods
Swan: Poems and Prose Poems

WINTER SOLSTICE

Sometimes it is the growing darkness
that writes the lines. How foolish we
are to think that we are not bound by
this. The red bird and I are animals. You
would admit to this too, I think. Short days
make for short foraging. It's not always
about food though. Sometimes, it's about
finding something else vital that you need to
sustain you. Survive. Joy, for example.

I know people who are starving.

I put out seed for the birds. I have enough to
share and their joy is mine. That's what the
short days are for—to realize that time is short.
We best receive what is offered and give joy.

"Come! Come! The feeder is full."

The sun is rising. Make thoughtful haste.

Lines Written in the Days of Growing Darkness
New York Times

DOGS WITHOUT LEASHES

Dogs have stories.
People have stories.

￼

I saw her in the morning, on one of those
sites on the internet. I had gone for two
months without a dog. That was enough.
In the afternoon, I drove to the shelter,
an hour and a half, and asked to meet her.

A middle-aged woman went to the back,
to the place of cement and shiny metal, of
kennel rows and forlorn once-they-were-wolves
singing out their deep grief and longings.

I waited.

The door opened. She slunk into the room
on her pink belly. I came to my knees
to greet her.

"Hello, pretty girl."

She urinated on the floor. I lifted my right hand
to the nape of her neck, and began stroking
her soft fur, black and white, all the while saying
lovely things. She trembled and tried to make
herself smaller than her bones were able to go.

Beneath my fingertips, under her tight skin, rolled
hard round pellets, several, put there by a shotgun blast.
Trapped there. Part of her body.

"May I take her for a walk?"

Outside, she strained to the end of the nylon leash,
wild-eyed, scanning the woods and fields,
planning the direction and speed she would go,
should she break from what tethers her to this world.

🐦

Whenever we go hiking, she runs out ahead of
me on the trail – up the mountain or down. Every
so often she'll stop, and look back, tongue lolling.

"Are you coming?!
Please, let's keep going!"

"Yes. I'm coming.
I'm coming, pretty girl."

She runs back down the path towards me, smiling,
coming nearly close enough for me to touch her, but
never close enough. There's a glint in her eye. Her tail
is wagging. She turns, and bolts off again, full speed
ahead, and around the next bend.

I watch her go.

🐦

When I went back into the lobby, the woman
behind the counter looked anxious, embarrassed,
perhaps, apologetic.

"We have lots of other dogs," she said.
"I can bring you several more to meet."

"No need," I said, handing her the adoption
form and the fee.

"We understand each other."

POND LILLIES

Do you ever wonder what Monet thought
of the lilies? The ones there in the dark-watered
pond on a summer's day. Those petals and pads
working their sweet way into his soul.

How is it that we have forgotten this art of
intimacy with the other? I stand here on the
edge, a thousand voices inviting me to go
deeper.

There are lilies floating.
White vessels for the sky.

Oh, yes, *what in this world is perfect?*
What resides without wanting to lead
us to the pain of knowing our true selves?

I think the answer is either nothing or everything.

I happen to be someone who finds perfection in
what is broken. How lovely.

A lily broke me open today.

The Ponds
House of Light

SPRING

Every year
when it comes,
I ask myself:

"What am I emerging from?"
"What am I emerging into?"

Sooner or later we must leave
the darkness. Ready or not
the brisk air of early spring
wants bodies to hold on to.

So, I think on the others coming forth.
The bear and her cubs that have been
hidden among the rock walls
above my cabin.

The frogs and salamanders that
were below ground,
breathing through their skin.

The flowers, a sacred pattern
of cells laid out on an invisible
blueprint of celebration.
And I have a question:

how too do I take myself into this world?
I think about how it seems
so effortless to them.
There they are where they
weren't before.

But poets like to find things,
like an idea,
like a meaning,
something that causes stirring,
because a world that always
sleeps cannot awaken.

So, this is it, I think:
some words on a page,
some questions arising among
them.

Here I am saying,

"It is spring!"
And asking you to notice
that something wants
to emerge,

and must.

IT WILL BE IN THE SILENCE

Sometimes you come upon a place that
beckons you into silence: an old stone bench,
a lake shore, a certain time in your life. Nothing
small can reside there.

I'm looking for that place now, the kind of place
that puts clocks to rest because something must
come forth to reset everything. I don't want to
follow these rules and constructs anymore,
written, not written, felt.

Something is asking me not to, and it is wise.

Reason doesn't have roots that run deep enough
to tap the place that I am longing for, that place
where obvious things cannot be explained. That
place that is called sacred even by those who
have never used the word before.

I want you to sit and wait with me, away from the
noise and the voices of those who speak only to rob
you of your name. What most needs to be heard
hasn't yet been said.

Such Silence
Blue Horses: Poems

LIVING

Everything that is me, cannot be
contained in one version of me,
cannot be contained at all,
really. There is so much in here
that wants to get out into the world
and try on a thousand—maybe
a million—ways of being. "What
do you do?" Oh, so many things.
So many wonderful things.

The Journey
Dream Work

SUFIS WHIRLING

I like to think about Sufis whirling, wondering
what they see, or if they see at all. Maybe,
there is something beyond seeing.

I think, perhaps, it is knowing. You,
understand, don't you?

Poets must have one foot in knowing and
the other in what is not knowable. That's our dance.

Where Does the Dance Begin, Where Does it End?
Why I Wake Early: New Poems

SUNRISE

What it says is this:

"You are here.
Make the most of it.
I'll offer you something,
but not much.
Lovely colors. A bright form.
An idea, perhaps.
You must be brilliant about it.
Make thoughtful observations.
Commit your heart.
Do something brave.
Make it an act of love.
You won't get this day again."

Sunrise
Dream Work

WHITE PINES

My little cabin is in what they call a holler. Here, the sun is slower to arrive than on the ridges. I prefer to meet it there rather than wait on the world's turning. Greeting the day is ritual. No, it is more than that, it is ceremony. The trees know this too, and I think also all those shrubs beneath them and the vines that use them to reach up to the heavens. Like me, climbing these mountains.

Often, the deer watch me, branches as masks. Today, it was a young white pine the doe chose. She didn't know that I knew the fawn was beside her, low in the dry stream bed, but I did. They walked on together and I, alone. What do I make of the rabbits in the grassy meadows? How are there so many, so complacent? Isn't this fox-certainty, coyote-certainty wonderful in the way that it teaches gratitude for clover and love of a moment?

Back to the white pine. There aren't many here. Not tall. Not dense. Mostly, they are young and spindly. It's like the artist had forgotten them and then suddenly said, "Oh, pines! There must be pines." Then he—or she—fit them into the remaining spaces because they are deserving. Five long needles each, that's how I know they are white pines. Of course, there are also the memories of buying them—white pines—for the dozen Christmases we were something called a family.

Once—well more than once—I sat with glorious children on a faraway mountain watching the sunset and the stars arrive, confident and twinkling. We counted them in three languages and sang songs that these same stars had taught their ancestors out of necessity. I don't remember the words, but I remember the laughter and how the night sky was caught up in their eyes. They didn't know darkness like I know darkness. I prayed they never would.

A walk isn't finished until the walker has acknowledged at least one great vulnerability and discovered something to be grateful for. I'm not talking about the pines. I am saying that maybe we should be more like artists, rabbits, and our ancestors' children.

White Pine
White Pine

THE ANGELS IN MY HEAD

I have angels in my head.
They teach me to be a better human
than I would be if left to this rather
awkward task alone.

They say things like:

Stop!
Look!
Listen!
Here, now!

They give me a chance. They nudge me
into remembering that there is a difference
between living and existing. Things exist.
I want to do better than that.

Sometimes they quarrel.
Quarreling angels make for interesting
company. Sometimes, there is just so
much good, so much loveliness, so much
wonderment to be experienced that
these angels feel the need to fight
for my attention.

I think this is what it means to be blessed.

LOONS ON A MAINE LAKE

When I was a young girl we went to a cabin
in Maine that belonged to Grandma Boo.
It sat beside a big lake. I don't remember
its name, but it was summer and I caught
dragonfly larvae—big darners—that left
their thin-shelled bodies behind on the porch
screens and so I escorted them—blue and
green with wings—into the large world on
the palm of my hand.

They chose the sky for company, but return,
sometimes, alighting in memories.

At dusk, misty twilight, the boys—teen or
maybe twentyish—next door skinny dipped,
diving in from the lip of their dock, swimming
to a pined island midway. I can still hear the
plunge—one, two. The rawness fascinated
me, awoke something.

So, I started swimming then too, short strokes
around the edges of our dock and catfish came
to me, like a gift, nibbling my toes, swirling—
silky—between my dog-paddling legs. Catfish.
There was something magical about those fish
and I never once wanted to catch them.

But, this story is actually about loons and how
they cried and vanished, appeared some place
else, and vanished again, and how they did
this for hours.

Even as a little girl I knew that I was
seeing my life:

How I would vanish
and how I must learn
to use my voice before
I do.

OBSERVATIONS

I wonder,

What do the wild geese, looking down,
think of us as they V northward in raucous
skeins at Winter's close?

And what are they saying?

And why have I not yet learned the
vocabulary of passing geese after so many
years of back-and-forths?

And, what good is a romantic notion if
no one ever gets kissed?

It feels something like that, don't you think?
The wild invites fullness and emptiness
in the same casual breath.

I have been wild. My soul remembers the
intuitively tenuous sound of that vow. Being
of the wild requires that we pledge ourselves
to authenticity:

A muskrat agrees to be an oily-haired muskrat.
The praying mantis dedicates its two front legs
to grabbing and holding and worshiping, and a
bird says, "yes," to being whatever species of
bird laid the egg that it pipped out of, one
"it-must-be-now" peck at a time, on that first
day of its life.

The World I Live In
Felicity

You must not waiver or doubt your destiny,
for everything else is depending on you to
keep your agreement. To show up. To do
what it is you do. And, generally speaking,
that will include dying to something larger
than yourself.

Yes, I wonder,

what the wild geese think of us as they V
northward in raucous skeins at Winter's close.

Perhaps they say to each other:

"See, down there,
the footprints upon the land?

"This is what it looks like when
a species breaks the promise."

And, meanwhile, here we are,
looking up and thinking:

"Oh, a flock of geese!

Oh, how wonderful it must be to be wild and free."

Wild Geese
Dream Work

PEOPLE IN WINTER

Foxes don't try to hide what it takes
to live. They see no reason for shame,
and so do their deeds in the bright of
moonlight, sometimes announcing them,
like the vixen did in the meadow two
nights after she took my golden rooster
by the neck.

In winter, there are two thieves:

The fox and the season trying
to steal the fox.

One of them succeeds.
You can't blame it.

Why do people look upon the angel
in the snow and say they are that?

Foxes in Winter
House of Light

I WOULD LIVE LIKE THIS

To me, the sunflowers are more meaningful
than gold and I once was in a wild home in
which the walls—and the ceiling—were filled
with honey. I can live like this, like everything
is expressing its desire to be of some service to
the soul of the world. I could put out a bowl for
the honey, yes. I could sell the sunflowers, yes.
But it is their pricelessness by which I want and
need to live. At least on most days, and I think
that is practical. There was, for example, in my
childhood, a rose-breasted grosbeak above a
stream. Its currency was awe, neither bought nor
sold. I do not have to contract with mockingbird
to be my advisor, nor a brook to be my muse.
Certainly, you must already know that the stars
shout out their names while playing giddy
games behind the clouds. Every picture that we
paint takes on a life of its own. I do agree that
it's an odd learning to make them into something
cheerful, but that's it, it can be done. I would live
like this: like money dulls in our eyes and the silver
of water is the bright shiny object of our greatest
affections.

How Would You Live Then?
Blue Iris

HENRY

"Who is he?" asked the beagle as Henry
stepped out of the car.

Henry, he said. He's had a hard life
and he's going to stay with us for awhile.

"Is he nice?" The beagle asked. "He's kinda
funny looking. I'm cute. He's simultaneously
handsome and ugly. How is that possible?"

Yes. He's different. Different can be special.
Good special. Please, be polite and say hello.

"Hello, Henry. That food bowl is mine. And,
that muddy place under the porch is mine too."

Henry: "I smell cats!"

The beagle: (to the man) "He's easily
distracted, isn't he?"

Henry thrust himself into the shrubs
and grabbed a stick.

The beagle put her nose to the ground and
started walking the fenceline, "I think he should
go back to that place."

Give him a chance. We all need a chance. Maybe
you can teach him something. You've been loved
all your life. He needs to learn to be loved.

The beagle looked up, raising her nose into the air, trying to make it seem like she'd just caught a scent. It was really an idea. She had an idea about Henry.

Time passed. Henry learned to focus, not quite like a beagle can focus, but something like that. Henry learned to be loved. Like the beagle and the man love each other.

Then the man said, it's time for Henry to go. He can have his own person now, someone who can love just him.

"I want to help," said the beagle. "I can tell his story."

"He's different. Different can be special."

You can love different.

THE WAY A FLOWER OPENS

Have you ever been kissed the way
a flower opens? Those with short lives
must know something of pleasure,
mustn't they? And beauty, whether
it be their own or they just choose
to find it everywhere. I think that
flowers must kiss bees, and butterflies,
and, yes, the heavenly air as much as
they dare. I won't say an unkind thing
about that.

I Know Someone
Felicity

SONG FOR SUMMER

In the days that creep toward summer,
have you noticed how the flowers
have become practiced at rising into
the sky and give no hint of the darkness
from which they emerged? They choose
to be bold. And do you think about the
trees hosting all the little cupped nests and
the little cupped nests holding something
precious that will have to make its way
into the world by taking a risk on an impossible
dream? Can you hear the humidity like I can
hear the humidity, coming alive, growing its own
body out of nothingness? Some people complain
about it, but not me. I know this shroud and
how a woman is to wear it. A dragonfly crosses
paths with a butterfly down by the pond
where the green frog sits edge-wise on
a stone in the sun. Into the night the bats take insects
on wing and the barred owls speak out the only
question they know. This is where I live: in this
place of welcoming and celebration. Summer is on
her way. I will meet her on the porch steps,
wearing my shroud.

Song for Autumn
New and Selected Poems, Volume Two

MOUNTAIN STREAM POEM

I've looked, but I cannot find a poem
that Mary Oliver has written about
a rushing mountain stream, the
kind that takes on the tongues
of gods after storms have done
their cleansing and prepared the
land for what is next to come. How
could she not? How could her pen not
have stopped here, so many times
before, wondered, listened, and then
told the stories that the gods want
us to hear, want us to live?

I have written one for her.

MY MOTHER WAS

My mother was the purple iris,
sometimes a peony, but never
the carnation. My mother was
red lipstick and a big, bright smile
that sometimes lied about how
much she loved her life. She counted
her burdens and could recite them
with ease, but she said that you
could make things better with a bag
of peanut M&Ms. Green ones, especially.
You don't forget, not all of it.

But when you bury someone
in a blue ceramic jar
near the old boxwoods
and walk away,
things start to become
hard to remember.

I don't know the meaning of life.
But, maybe, it is simply to take notice.

Flare
The Leaf and the Cloud

THE SNAKE

Judge me to be a vile trickster, a low
life. Project all your fears onto me.
These things, I can shed.

Accept my invitation to place the belly
of your entire being on the skin of
the Earth, to undulate, sensuously,
across the terrain of the divine feminine,
to understand this place, your place,
our place.

There is a gateway to heaven.

The Snake
House of Light

PONIES

You wonder if this world will grow kinder eventually,
if there is a piece of some yet-lingering God inside each of us
that has a desire to make something beautiful, or
something beautiful happen, even a little something.

The ponies must have known how the veil had thinned,
how they had already become meat and glue and hide in
the eyes of the auctioneer. "How much to end these
lives?" Bid. Bid high. Sold.

The slaughter truck's gate-mouth was wide open, its belly
waiting to be filled with the sound of hooves on metal,
fear: its acrid scent, and questions about what a soul
is worth on any given day.

That's not beautiful. For God's sake, it is not.

Do you want to cry? I do cry. Does your heart sink and
crumble because you struggle to live in a world
that has coined pain as currency? I struggle.

The stockyard was growing eerily quiet when they left,
the trailer gate locked behind them, no choices of their
own available. Owned.

In truth, I wasn't actually there to see it. Someone told me
the story about a month later, on the day that I went to meet
the lovely ponies and place kisses on their soft muzzles.
There was so much life in their eyes.

You see, the Gods had conspired to get a few strangers and a few dollars together, and something beautiful happened.

I wonder about kindness, and what else it can do.

Franz Marc's Blue Horses
Blue Horses

THIS NIGHT THE RAIN SPOKE TO ME

This night
the rain
spoke to me
heavy, saying,

"I will create
a place for holding
lovers and their spawn,

and you will be happy
with this earthly life."

And, it kept its promise
and dropped.
For hours.

And, the night smelled
like spring, like yearning,
like sex. Like life hell
bent on renewal.

And, I listened to all
the voices crying out
in the darkness
and understood

everything they
said.

And, some part of me
was very happy.

Last Night the Rain Spoke to Me
What Do We Know: Poems and Prose Poems

THOSE WHO BOW THEIR HEADS

I too want to keep the company of those
who bow their heads. What is our
purpose if it is not attentiveness
and gratitude? Let us have allegiances
with that which breaks us open and
that which makes us whole.

Have you noticed how the light finds
you, but always gives you over to the
darkness so that you can see what is
really there to see? Listen to the voices
around you, I have begged, how they tell
you about humanity in gestures. Your
humanity, theirs, mine, ours. How much
of it we have neglected out of neglect of
this generous world. I want to comfort
this place with a million utterances of,

"Thank you!"

Let me find other words too, always, and
walk with reciprocity in my step. Always.
If we were having dinner together tonight,
I'd say something simple like:

"There is food on the plate.
Lives have made it so."

That's plenty of reason, certainly you
agree, to bow our heads in attentiveness
and in gratitude.

"Thank you!"

"Thank you!"

THE NECESSARY VOYAGE

When the birds have come to say, "wake and rise,"
I do, gathering my life into a bundle of severances,
resting words of gratitude on the brows of the departed,
some of them in mirrors, my heart used up in this place.

Not of all voyagers get maps or a compass that points
to something other than grief. Some must go without
bearing. Actually, the honest books, sermons, and town
criers say that many and many more are going this way,
just on from somewhere destroyed, hoping with an acrid,
musty hope that there is a healing land before them.
For a man to leave what he loves, there's a good chance
he's already died, or begun to and surely will.

Does one remain a citizen of a fallen city?
Shall I ask this of the woodland creatures? Shall I ask it
of my name and those who carried it into the world
before me over long distances because, well, because
love departed the soul of some person and place.

At my desk near a large picture window, I write and
and wonder while listening to the song of birds
who will soon lift and go. What can I inherit of this?
What's there to make of the necessary voyage when
the land no longer offers a tending embrace.

I don't know how the birds do it, keeping their glee
about it year after year. We humans aren't built
like that it seems. Life after life it goes on, the
wretched longing for birth place, for story place,
for the place that made sense of us.

We arrive wounded, betrayed by the gods, weeping,
and impatient to love and be loved again. Looking
around I realize that we are all necessary voyagers.
How do I make my peace with that fact? How
do I reconcile my ability to hang seed for the birds,
but not to provision water in a desert, or a map and
compass to the great ship captain?

WE ARE KIND OF LIKE THAT

Sometimes I am saddened by the need for us.
Why must a poet be called to this place
that is so evidently filled with grace and
not the smallest amount of grandeur?

Our words say:

"Stop for a moment! Shush; get quiet! Listen, closely!
There are blessings calling out for your attention.
Right here. Right now. Within, and around you."

I suppose people expect blessings to be
bright, shiny things. Most of the time,
they are not. They are quite ordinary looking.
They require a closer introspection, a deeper
listening to be found.

We are kind of like that, you know.

Dogfish
Dreamwork

SO MANY

The frogs are so many
you can't mistake the pond for emptiness.
Each voice, different, like a moment.
And I stop my hurrying, for awhile.
What fortune it is to awaken each morning!
I go to the ponds, anticipating something
miraculous at the edge of what is solid and
what is not. And, it is there, something,
always there to greet the unknown day,
and I wonder if my coming isn't its story
of something ordinary but worthy of
words. Maybe, I'm lucky and it's praise.

I'm praising them, all of them, so many
of them, now here calling out for what they want.
Look at that! How they know it and say it.
"Come to me! Come to me!" Have any of us
ever been that bold, truly?
Imagine that in your own body! Really
saying what you want and need.

Surely, I will praise them as they float on the pond
and tell it as it is!
This day is worthy of their gusto, of their intent
to say "Yes!" with bravado to the forces
rushing through them. Life!
Sometimes I forget about it. About what a
chance this is. What a chance to live, and call out
for what you really want, for what brings you alive.
This is my frog voice.

One
Why I Wake Early: New Poems

SO THIS FEAR

"So this is fear," I say when the stand is taken.

"So this is fear," I say when the next stand is taken.

Have you ever seen love take a stand?

Kneel. I have seen love kneel.

MOCKINGBIRD IN WINTER

All winter, Mockingbird, in his steel-gray
suit, perches atop the tangled thicket of
multiflora rose, swallowing bright red
rose hips and awaiting the next blessed moment,
brief as it may be, when the sun stirs
a drowsy insect awake and into a fine death.

It's a rather odd thing to watch him in silence,
mine and his. We both have so much to
say, and hearts that have forgotten need translators.
I wonder about words pulled from the voice of
the world and words pulled from within.
Are they so different?

You give us the instruction:

"Pay attention.
Be astonished.
Tell about it."

I'm sitting with that, as the mockingbird sits not
far from my window pane, fluffed and
elegant, and fully aware that I am watching him.
And, maybe too, he knows that I am wondering.

It can be hard to speak without contempt for
this self-led world, but he does it all summer long.
And, I try my best.

What is it like to shake off shell fragments and become the great celebrator of life?

I think the mockingbird needs another name.

And I want to tell it to the world.

THESE BONES

It seems that I am forever
trying to fall in love with
these bones, and the flesh
that keeps them hidden
away so that they might remain
mostly unspeakable.

This is your story too, if you are
honest about it. Being human.

When I was a little girl, my mother dressed
me in brightly colored bathing suits so that
I could be spotted way down the beach;
even then, I had a penchant for wandering.

I bent over sand buckets to identify shells for
delighted old ladies and gentleman, handed
sharks' teeth to astonished little boys,
but gathered the round, white vertebrae of
ocean-going fish for myself; a wild child seeks
adornment from the sea.

All you need is some string and you
can make a necklace.

And, there have been other bones:

Turtles left to the elements at roadside,
the deer the hunters lost to forest secrets,
dogs piled high at the end of an old road in

the middle of nowhere on a day that I had dedicated
to being charmed by birdsong and birds,

and I have visited museums, many of them,
where bones stare back at you, begging you to
remember a life that you never knew, to
imagine something when it was ensouled
and might have chosen to eat you for being so
close, or it might have run. But, it wouldn't
have stayed, not like this. Not this still, forever.

These other things are so easy to love, like this
stark day with the sycamores bearing their ribs.

They say that poems should have good bones.
Stories can be ligaments and tendons.

I wonder what our Mother feels in that moment
when we walk away from her for the very
first time,

and later when she hears us remark:

"I have been abandoned."

How easily we abandon ourselves
to stories in which we do not belong.

Here, on Earth, we live such a story.
Being human.

I love all the old stories – the ancient ones –
in which ancestors are more than just bones,

just bones,

especially when the ancestors were not
just human like they are now,

in our way of speaking of

the world as not needing us.

Maybe, someone will adorn
themselves with these bones,
my bones.

It could, perhaps,
be me.

WHAT IT IS

This is a statement about things gone missing.
This is a reflection on beauty and how it is fleeting,
       and how memories can never be true
       to what we are gifted in any particular moment.
This is a call out to those still here, especially
those who know it. Those who are grateful.
This is an invitation to live. To cherish.
This is a reminder that you don't get forever.

What This is Not
Felicity

ACKNOWLEDGMENTS

Deep gratitude to Mary Oliver for lifting the words into the world that started the conversation and to Nature, our shared muse. Each of her poems that inspired is credited, along with the relevant collection, following each of my poems. All lines first published in a poem by Mary Oliver are demarcated in italics. The opening quote is from an interview posted on the Mary Oliver Facebook page on October 16, 2014.

Many thanks to Jason Kirkey for production assistance, Meredith McKnown Peyton (Peyton House Portraits) for contributing her photographic talents, and Len Fleischer for assisting with final edits. A deep bow to all of you who have welcomed my poems into your lives. You are greatly appreciated.

Love yourself. Then forget it.
Then, love the world.
−MARY OLIVER
To Begin With, the Sweet Grass
Evidence: Poems

ABOUT THE AUTHOR

Jamie K. Reaser has a passion for bringing people into their hearts, inspiring the heartbeat of community and, ultimately, empowering people to live with a heart-felt dedication to Mother Earth. Her award-winning writing explores the inter-relatedness of Nature and human nature. Jamie's collections of poetry include, *Huntley Meadows: A Naturalist's Journal in Verse*, *Note to Self: Poems for Changing the World from the Inside Out*, *Sacred Reciprocity: Courting the Beloved in Everyday Life*, *Wild Life: New* and *Selected Poems*, *Winter: Reflections by Snowlight*, and *Coming Home: Learning to Actively Love this World*. She is a Fellow of the International League of Conservation Writers.

Jamie makes her home at Ravens Ridge Farm in the Blue Ridge Mountains of Virginia.

Selected poems can be found on the Talking Waters poetry blog at www.talkingwaters-poetry.blogspot.com or through Talking Waters on Facebook.

CPSIA information can be obtained
at www.ICGtesting.com
Printed in the USA
BVHW032343160919
558630BV00001B/15/P